GREAT AMERICAN

HORSES

AN IMAGINATION LIBRARY SERIES

SADDLEBREDS

by Victor Gentle and Janet Perry

Gareth Stevens Publishing
A WORLD ALMANAC EDUCATION GROUP COMPANY

This book is dedicated to Tom Bass, whose life inspired us to reach beyond what people say about training horses, to what good trainers do.

—Victor Gentle and Janet Perry

Please visit our web site at: www.garethstevens.com
For a free color catalog describing Gareth Stevens' list of high-quality books and multimedia programs, call 1-800-542-2595 (USA) or 1-800-461-9120 (Canada).
Gareth Stevens Publishing's Fax: (414) 332-3567.

Library of Congress Cataloging-in-Publication Data

Gentle, Victor.
    Saddlebreds / by Victor Gentle and Janet Perry.
        p. cm. — (Great American horses: an imagination library series)
    Includes bibliographical references (p. 23) and index.
    ISBN 0-8368-2938-7 (lib. bdg.)
    1. American saddlebred horse—Juvenile literature. [1. American saddlebred horse.
    2. Horses.] I. Perry, Janet, 1960- II. Title.
    SF293.A5G46   2001
    636.1'3—dc21   2001020847

First published in 2001 by
Gareth Stevens Publishing
A World Almanac Education Group Company
330 West Olive Street, Suite 100
Milwaukee, WI 53212 USA

Text: Victor Gentle and Janet Perry
Page layout: Victor Gentle, Janet Perry, and Scott M. Krall
Cover design: Renee M. Bach
Series editor: Katherine J. Meitner
Picture researcher: Diane Laska-Swanke

Photo credits: Cover, pp. 5, 7, 9, 13, 17, 22 © Bob Langrish; p. 11 © CORBIS; p. 15 (both) Courtesy of Audrain County Historical Society Museums; p. 19 Photofest; p. 21 © Doug Shiflet

Printed in the United States of America

1 2 3 4 5 6 7 8 9 05 04 03 02 01

Front cover: Saddlebred and partner polishing up their performance in the field.

TABLE OF CONTENTS

Words that appear in the glossary are printed in **boldface** type the first time they occur in the text.

BRED TO SHINE

Saddlebreds are the showiest horses in North America. Even when they are walking in their fields, they hold their heads high and move their legs quickly. They always look as if they are leading a parade. With their ears pointed forward, their eyes gleaming, and their bodies perfectly shaped, they look like movie stars.

Most Saddlebreds have talents that trainers polish during months of hard work. That is why Saddlebreds sparkle when they perform. Their star qualities are **bred** into them — into their bones, their blood, and their hearts. They are designed to be spectacular show horses.

Even at a young age, this fine Saddlebred is showing off, with his neck beautifully arched, head held high, and feet lifted in a nice trot.

PACESETTING BREED

Saddlebreds get their elegance from some of the finest British horse **breeds**. Galloway and Hobby Horses were the first British horses brought to the American colonies. These riding horses were small and hardy with an easy **pacing gait**.

For several generations, the best Galloway and Hobby Horses were bred together. The result was a **harness** and riding breed known as the Narragansett Pacer.

Narragansett Pacers were strong enough to pull plows. Because of the Pacers' easy **gait**, riders could travel comfortably on long journeys. Even if they worked hard during the week, Pacers still looked handsome for Sunday visits to the neighbors.

This **mare**'s muscular body and arching neck are perfectly copied onto her **foal**.

STARS FOREVER

By 1776, American landowners had created a unique breed known as the "American horse," the "Kentucky saddler," or "saddle horse." They bred the most beautiful **mares** and **stallions** to each other or to a Morgan horse with star quality. By 1850, the **foundation sires** for the Saddlebred Horse breed had been born. Their names were Gaines' Denmark and Harrison Chief.

Throughout the 1800s, saddle horses were bred more for intelligence and style than for sturdiness. They were bred to be celebrities in horse shows and on the battlefield.

Wearing a splashy coat patched with black and white, a beautiful paint Saddlebred sails over the fence.

BELOVED STEED

Saddlebreds were ridden by generals and leaders in the American Civil War. One of the most famous friendships between a person and a horse was between General Robert E. Lee and Traveller.

Traveller was one of the finest horses ever. He had a black mane and tail, a silvery gray coat, dark eyes, and a beautiful head. He was gentle and smart.

He was also known far and wide — and traveled there, too! He stepped proudly in bumpy fields, ate trampled grass, and got little sleep. One time he reared just in time to miss a cannon ball, saving himself and General Lee from death. When Lee died, Traveller walked behind the casket at his funeral — an empty saddle on his back.

Confederate General Lee said, "Traveller is my only companion. He and I, whenever practical, wander out in the mountains and enjoy sweet confidences."

"RACK ON!"

Lee and Traveller may have lost the war, but they were a winning team — and being part of a winning team is what Saddlebreds do best. Saddlebreds are beautiful all on their own. With good training, they can be magnificent.

Saddlebreds are either three-gaited or five-gaited. Three-gaited Saddlebreds walk, trot, and canter in shows. Five-gaited Saddlebreds can also do the rack and the slow gait. The rack is a fast four-beat gait that goes left hind foot, left forefoot, right hind foot, right forefoot. The slow gait has the same foot order as the rack but is slower.

When "Rack on!" sounds in the show ring, Saddlebreds strut their stuff with strength and style.

To teach the rack and slow gait, the trainer leans her weight so that the horse has to put its feet in the proper order. This is the rack in action.

ALL THE KING'S HORSES

Tom Bass was born as a slave in Missouri in 1859. He worked his whole life gently training show horses to be spectacular. Queens, presidents, and other famous people admired his performances.

Many of the Saddlebreds that Bass trained became world famous. Miss Rex became the world champion Saddlebred at the Columbian Exposition in Chicago, Illinois, in 1893. "Buffalo Bill" Cody bought Bass' horse Columbus for his Wild West Show. Belle Beach, the last great show horse that Bass trained, could do every complicated step and gait of any horse in the world — and more.

Tom Bass was the best horse trainer in the world. He was called "king of the American horse show."

Main: Bass and Belle Beach do a little show for the camera. Inset: A formal portrait of Tom Bass.

A RECORD OF GREATNESS

On April 7, 1891, a man named Charles F. Mills created the Saddlebred horse **registry**, the first breed registry in the United States.

To be registered, Saddlebreds must be related to stallions called foundation sires. Mills chose Gaines' Denmark as the foundation sire in 1891. In 1991, the registry added a second foundation sire, Harrison Chief. Both were chosen because of their **conformation**.

Gaines' Denmark and Harrison Chief both had short backs, broad chests, and legs that were straight and strong. They got these traits from their British and American Morgan Horse ancestors.

These Saddlebred yearlings are elegantly built. Their legs are straight and long, their backs are nicely built, and their faces are handsome.

STAR QUALITY

Saddlebreds sparkle — so it is no wonder that many are movie stars. One black Saddlebred with a white star between his eyes became very famous. His name was Highland Dale.

In the 1940s and 1950s, Highland Dale was the starring "actor" in the movies *Black Beauty*, *Gypsy Colt*, and *Giant*. He was also the star in the TV series *Fury*. He usually played a wild stallion who could only be tamed and ridden by a good friend. In real life, Highland Dale was a gentle horse who easily learned new tricks and worked hard for long hours.

Here, Highland Dale rears in his most famous role — a horse named Fury. His fellow actor is not worried, because this is all an act.

AND THE WINNER IS . . .

Imperator, or "Perry," was a five-gaited Saddlebred who became the World's Grand Champion four years in a row. *The American Saddlebred* magazine said that while Perry was "not the best athlete," his audiences loved him, and he loved their applause. "He seemed to say, 'Look at me! I'm the best, and I'm having fun!'" Perry loved to perform.

In 1985, Perry was the first Saddlebred to win a place in the Hall of Champions. When he was older, he lived at the Kentucky Horse Park, where his fans could visit him.

Like all Saddlebreds, Perry sparkled. Like Perry, all Saddlebreds are born to be stars.

Perry racks round the ring with trainer Don Harris. Harris says, "You could tell by the look of him that he was a great horse — a natural."

DIAGRAM AND SCALE OF A HORSE

Here's how to measure a horse with a show of hands.
Head held high, here is a star-quality Saddlebred.

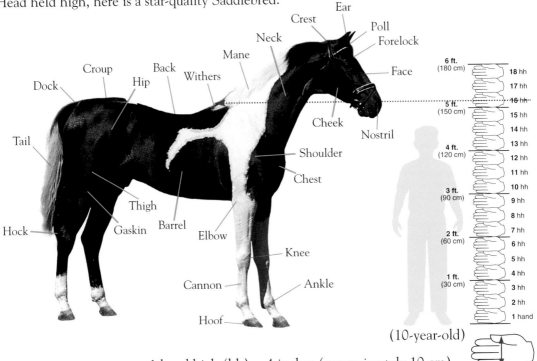

Ear
Crest
Poll
Neck
Forelock
Mane
Withers
Back
Face
Croup
Hip
Dock
Cheek
Nostril
Tail
Shoulder
Chest
Thigh
Hock
Gaskin
Barrel
Elbow
Cannon
Knee
Ankle
Hoof

6 ft. (180 cm)
5 ft. (150 cm)
4 ft. (120 cm)
3 ft. (90 cm)
2 ft. (60 cm)
1 ft. (30 cm)

18 hh
17 hh
16 hh
15 hh
14 hh
13 hh
12 hh
11 hh
10 hh
9 hh
8 hh
7 hh
6 hh
5 hh
4 hh
3 hh
2 hh
1 hand

(10-year-old)

1 hand high (hh) = 4 inches (approximately 10 cm)

WHERE TO WRITE OR CALL FOR MORE INFORMATION

American Saddlebred Horse Association
4093 Iron Works Parkway
Lexington, KY 40511
Phone: (606) 259-2742

MORE TO READ AND VIEW

Books (Fiction):   *Louisiana Blue: The Story of an Impassioned Girl Who Stops at Nothing When Her American Saddlebred Is in Danger.* Coleen Hubbard (Gareth Stevens)

Books (Nonfiction):   *The Complete Guides to Horses and Ponies* (series). Jackie Budd (Gareth Stevens)
From Slave to World-Class Horseman: Tom Bass. J. L. Wilkerson (Acorn)
Great American Horses (series). Victor Gentle and Janet Perry (Gareth Stevens)
United States Pony Club Manual of Horsemanship: Basics for Beginners. Susan E. Harris (Hungry Minds)

Magazines: *Horse Illustrated* and its new magazine for young readers, *Young Rider*

Videos (Nonfiction):   *Biography: Robert E. Lee.* (A&E Biography)
Noble Horse. (National Geographic)
The Real Cowboy: Portrait of an American Icon. (Discovery Communications)

WEB SITES

American Saddlebred Horse Association:
www.asha.net/youth.html

For more information on Saddlebred Horses:
www.american-saddlebred.com

For general horse information:
www.henry.k12.ga.us/pges/kid-pages/horse-mania/index.htm
www.saluki.com/baghdad/saddlbrd.htm
www.ansi.okstate.edu/breeds/horses

Some web sites stay current longer than others. To find additional web sites, use a reliable search engine, such as Yahooligans or KidsClick! (http://sunsite.berkeley.edu/KidsClick!/), with one or more of the following key words to help you locate information about horses: *canter*, *Columbian Exposition*, *horse gaits*, *Imperator*, *Saddlebred Horses*, and *Tom Bass.*

GLOSSARY

You can find these words on the pages listed. Reading a word in a sentence helps you understand it even better.

bred (past tense of breed) (v) — to have chosen a stallion and a mare with certain features to make foals with similar features 4, 6, 8

breed (n) — horses that share features as a result of careful selection of stallions and mares to produce foals 6, 8, 16

conformation (KON-for-MAY-shun) — the way a horse's body is built 16

foal — a baby horse 6

foundation sire — a male horse, or one of the male horses, from which all horses in a breed must be descended 8, 16

gait — a way of moving. Walking, running, pacing, trotting, and cantering are examples of horses' gaits 6, 12, 14, 20

harness — straps that wrap around a horse's body and attach to a wagon, cart, or buggy so that the horse can pull it 6

mare — an adult female horse 6, 8

pacing gait — a gait where the legs move together, one side first and then the other 6

registry (REJ-iss-tree) — a certain group of rules set by a group of breeders, formally listing which horses belong to the breed 16

stallion — an adult male horse 8, 16, 18

INDEX